Hedgehogs Coloring Book For Adults

This book belongs to:

_____

Copyright © 2017 Hedgehogs Coloring Books

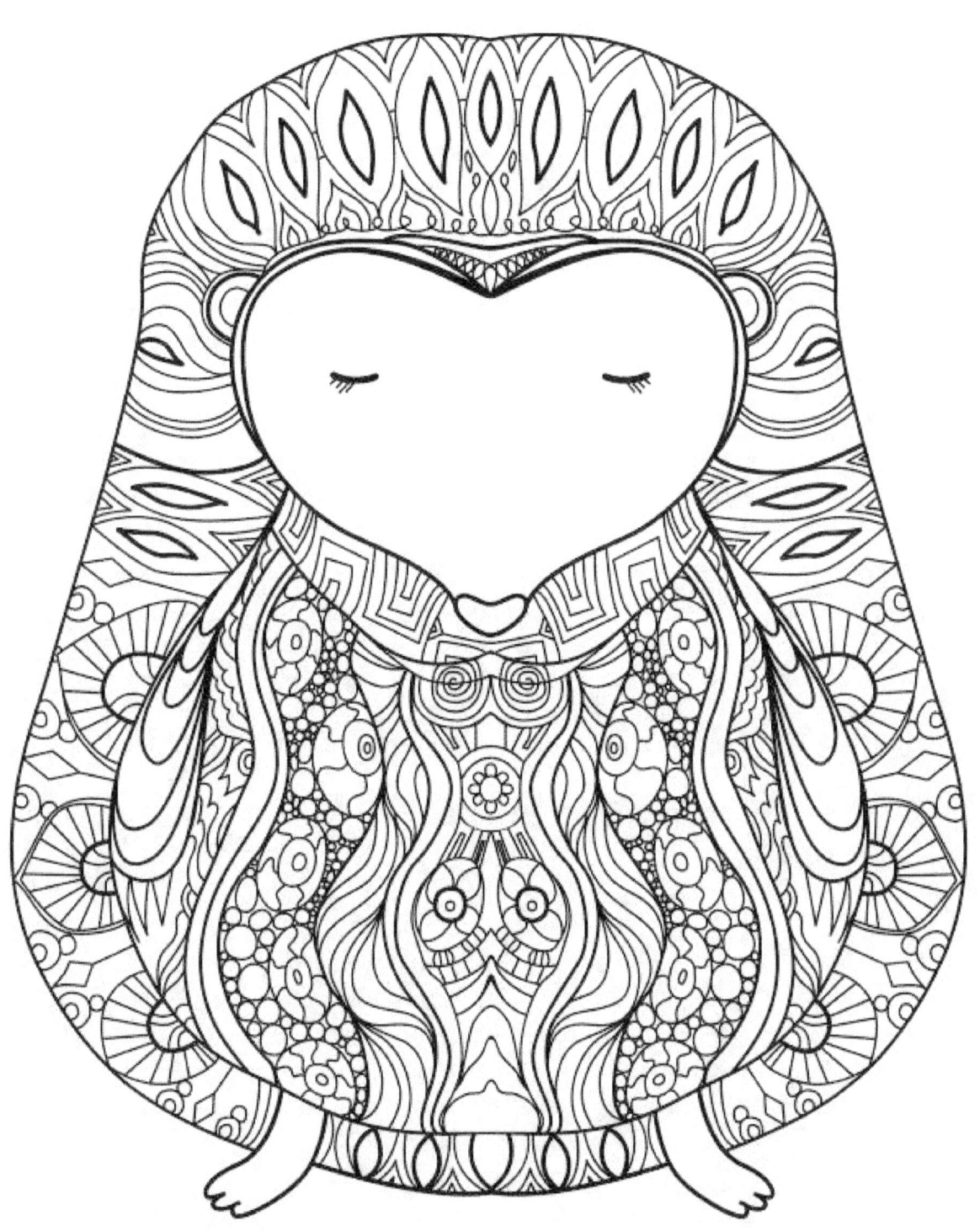

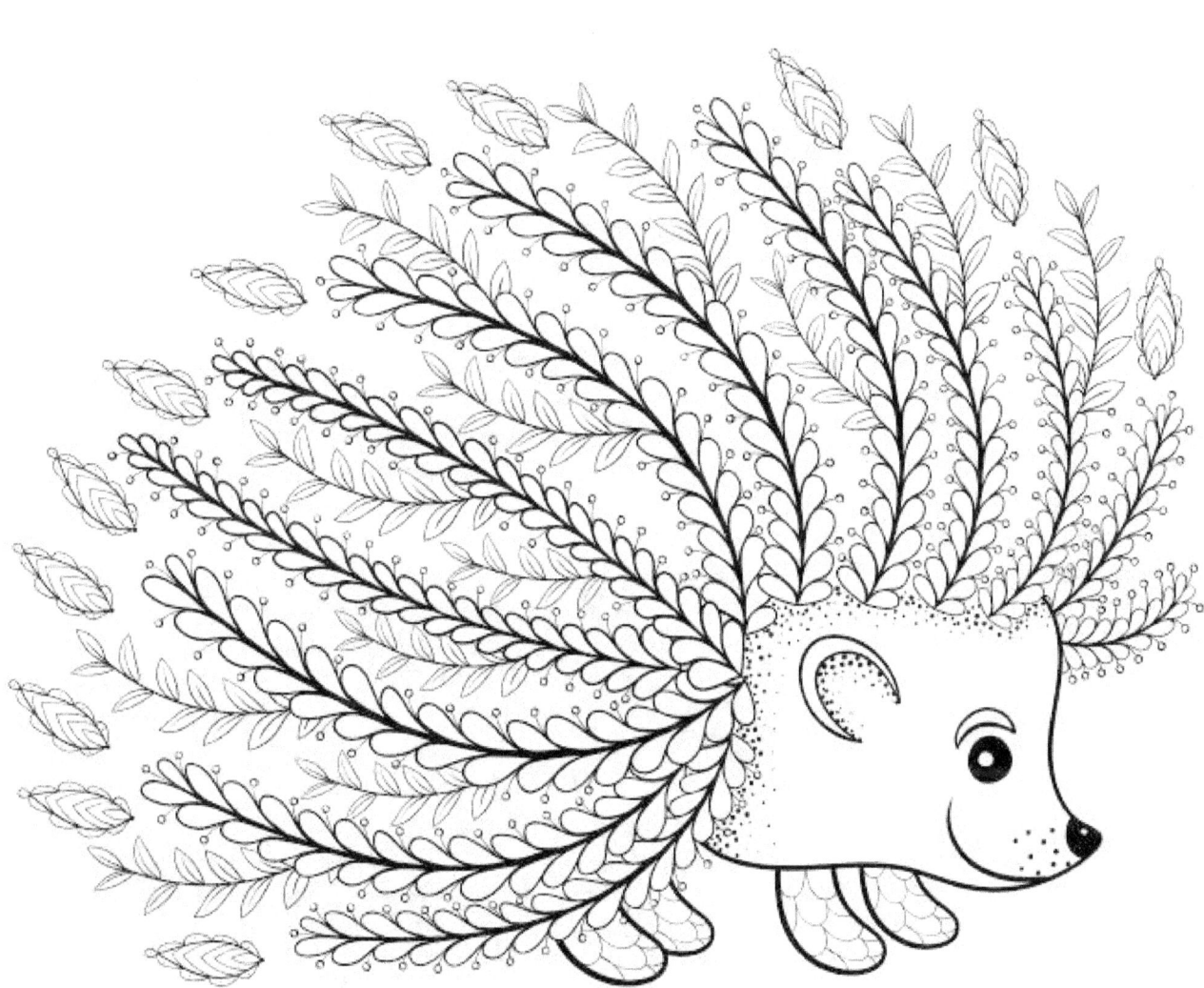

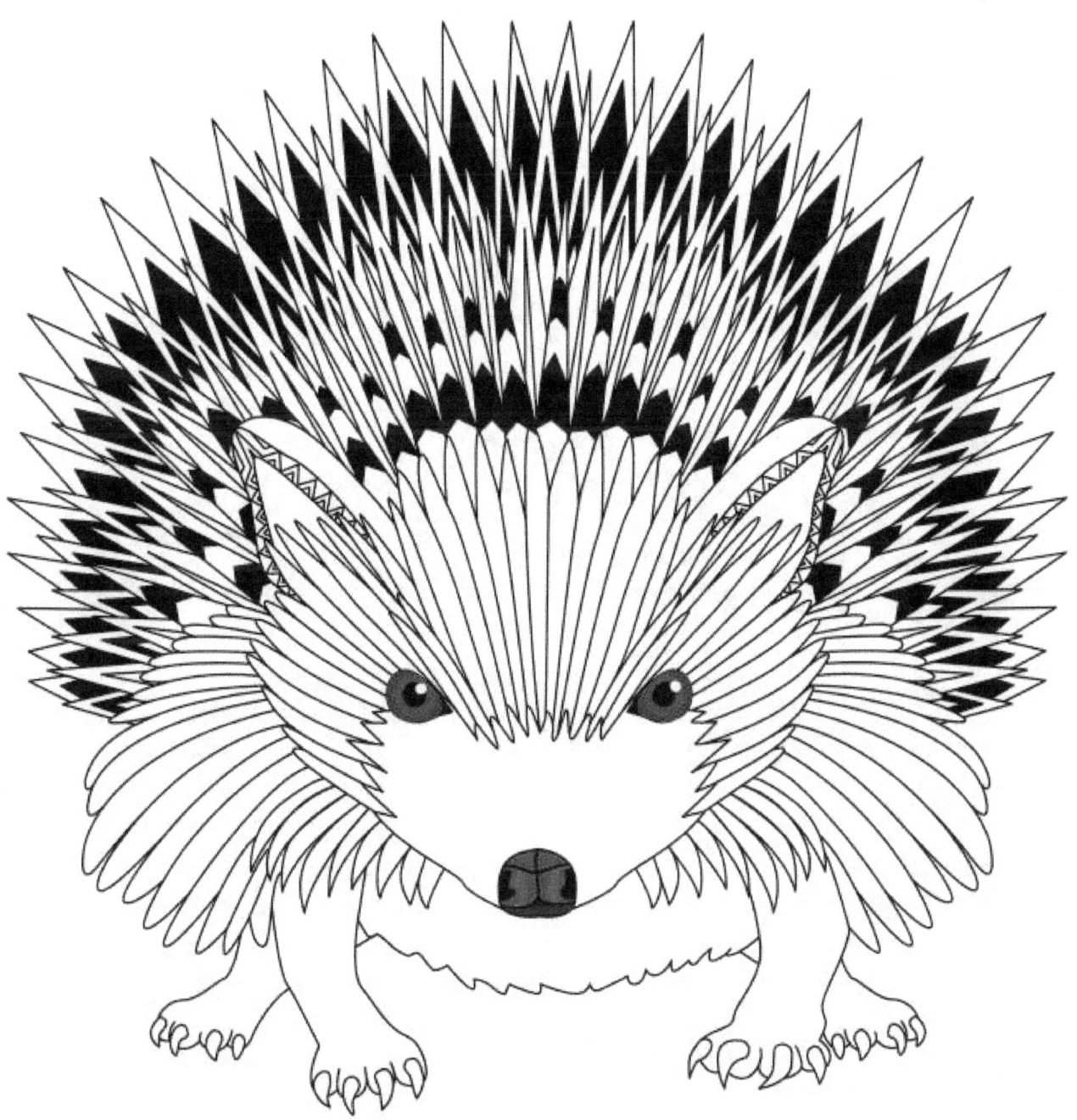

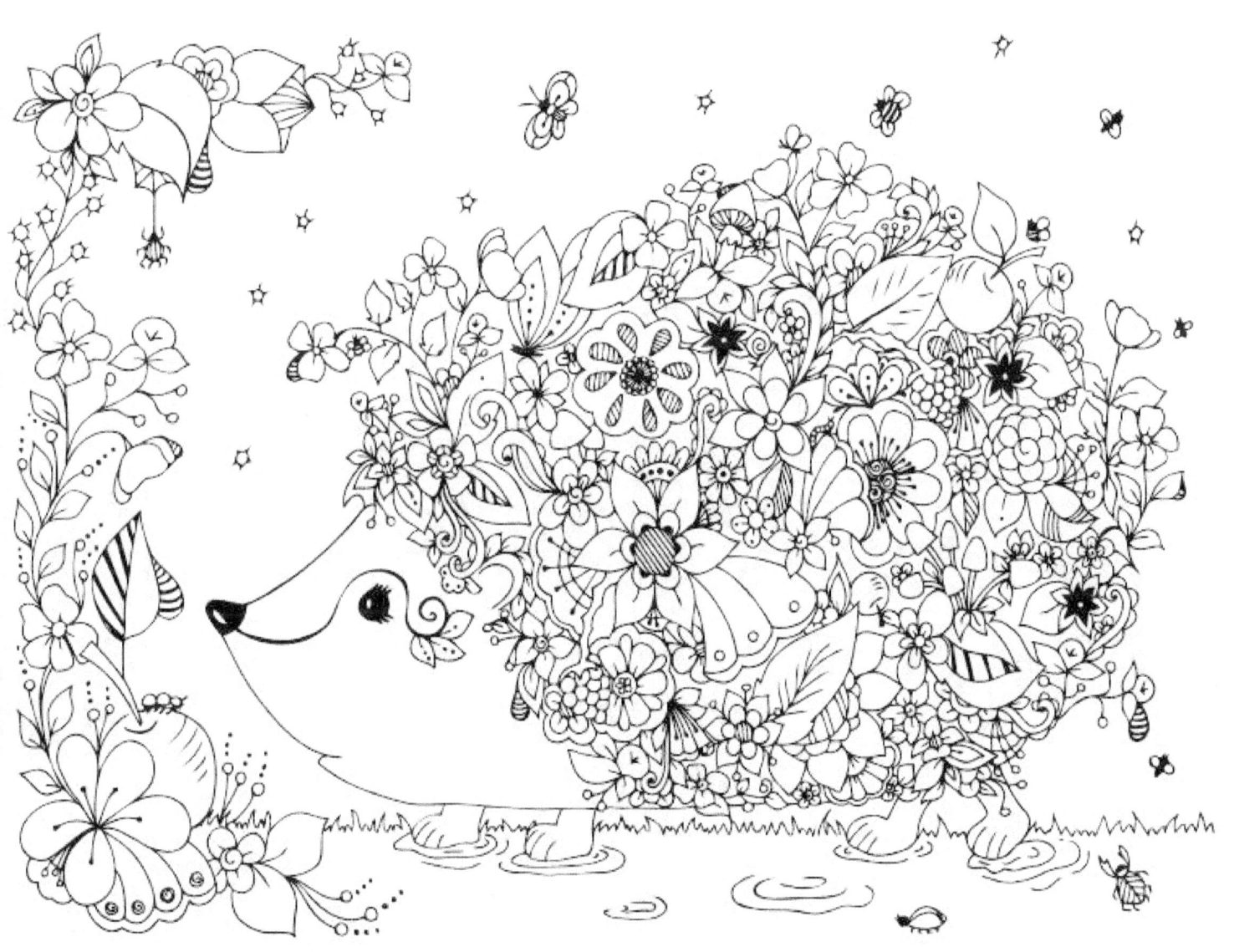

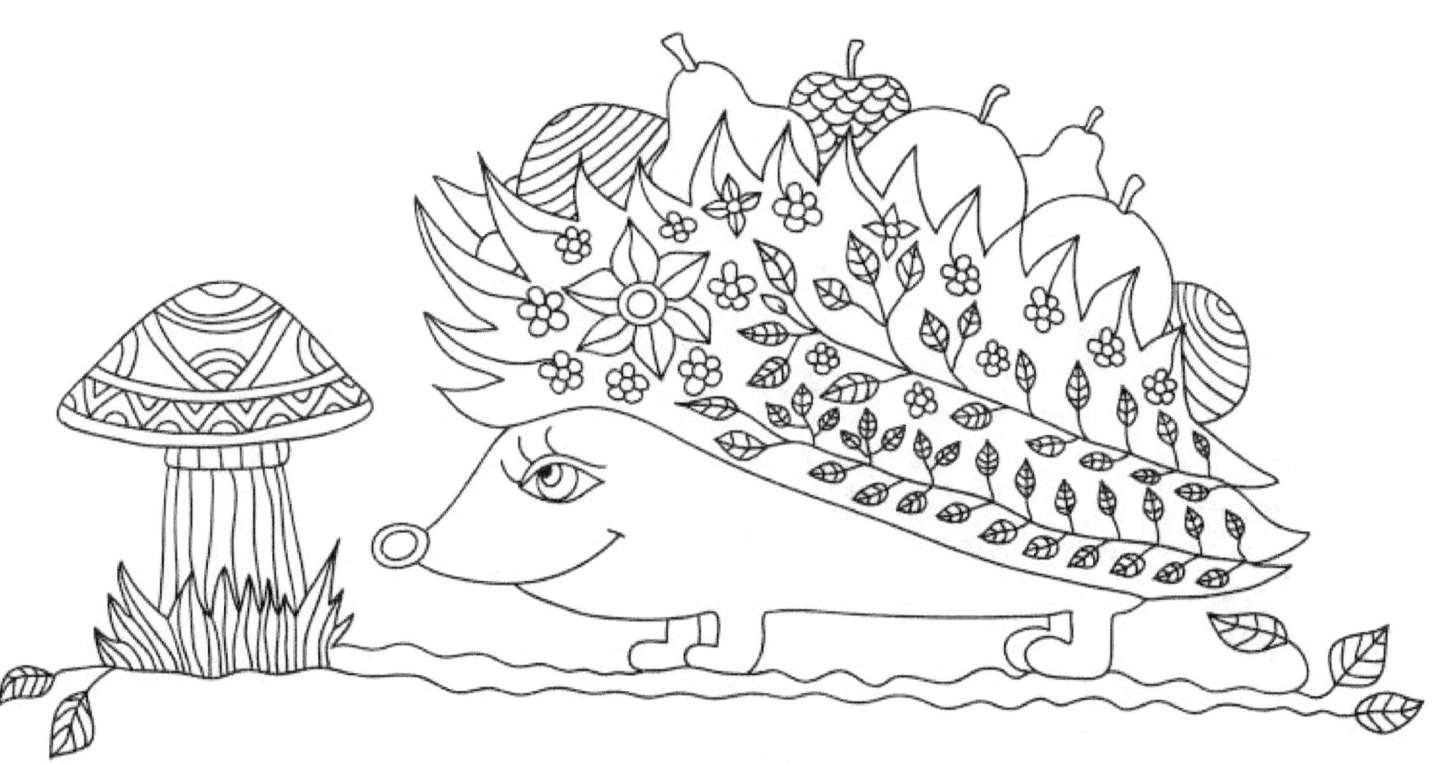

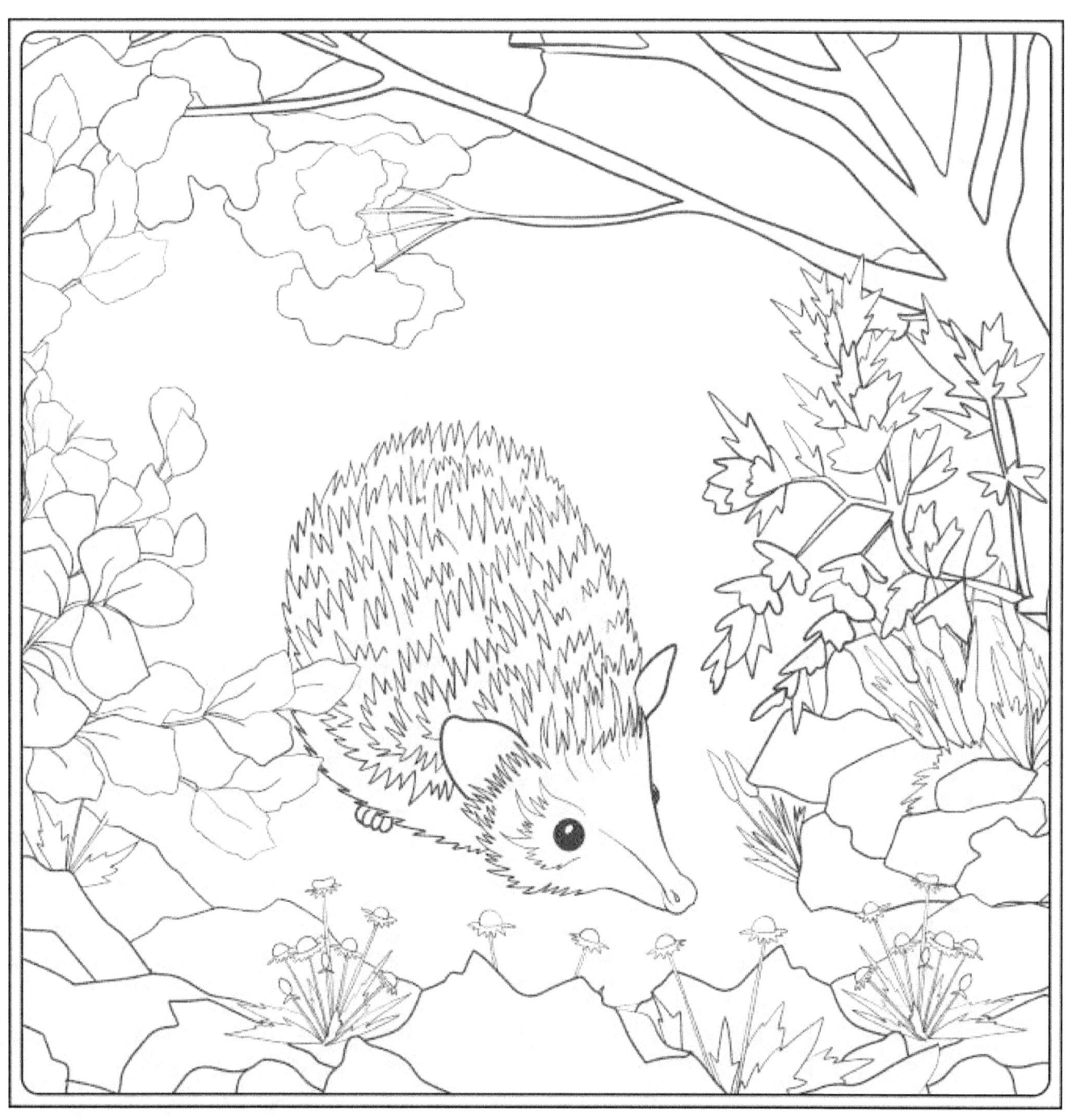

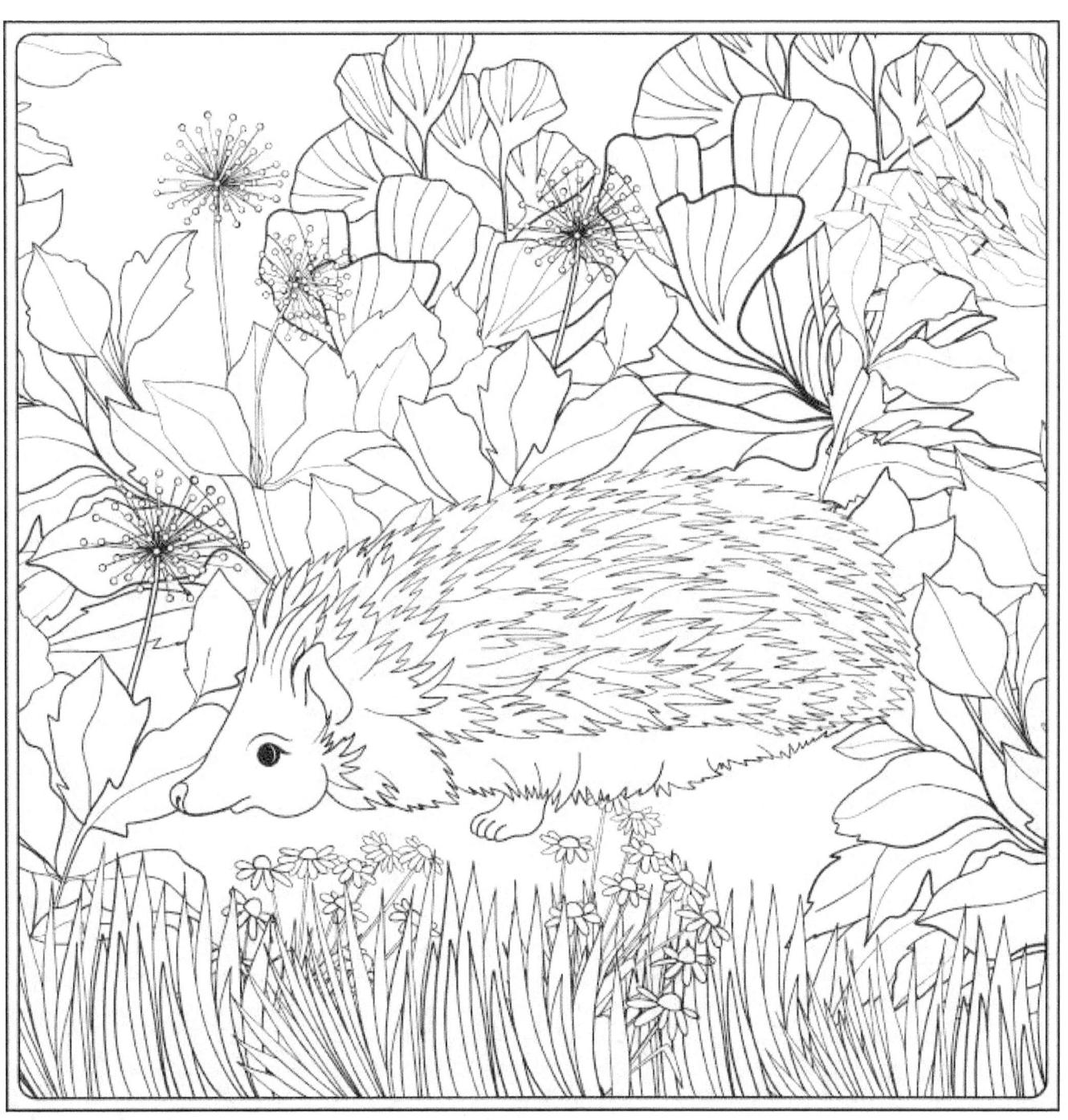

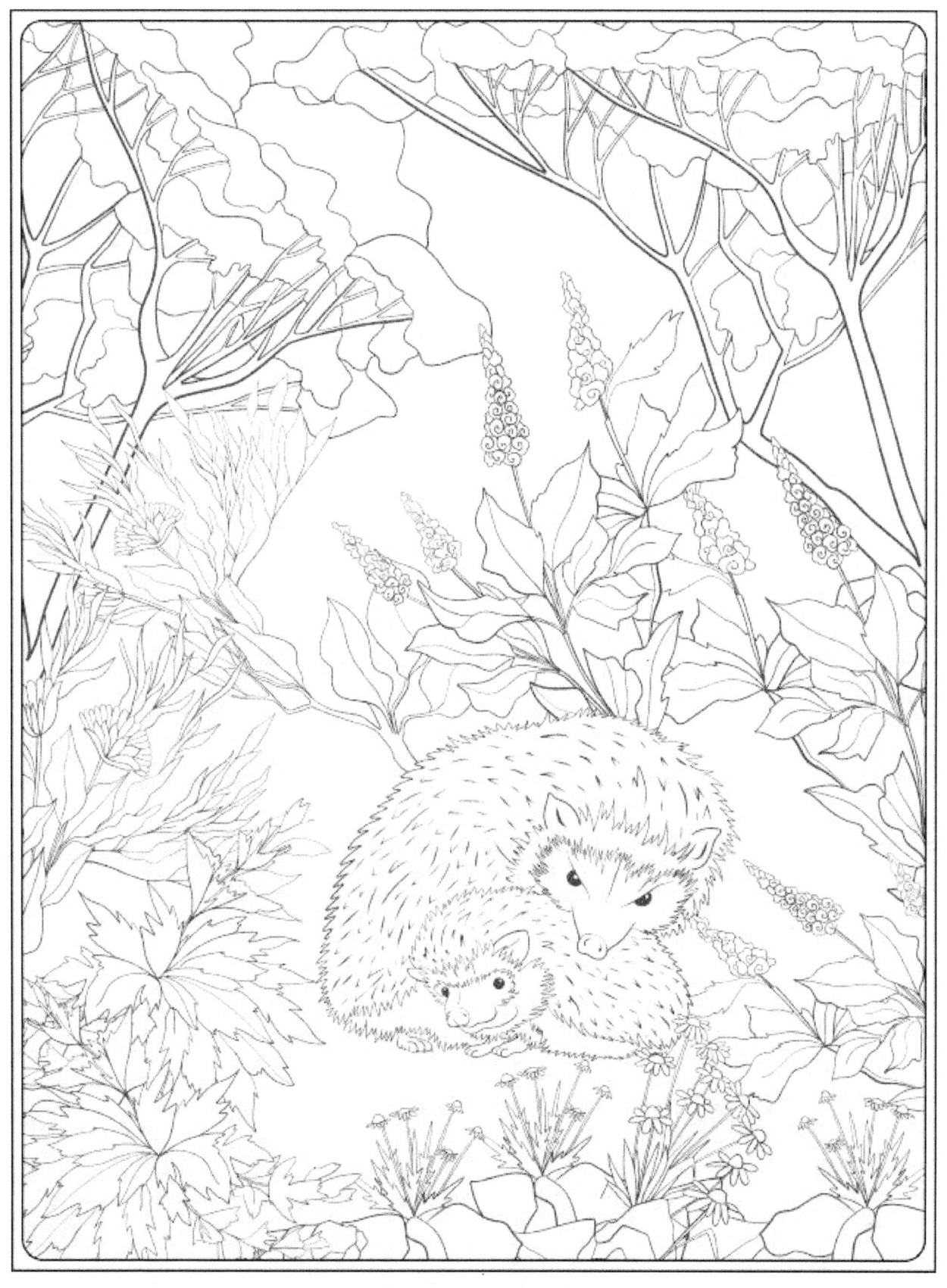

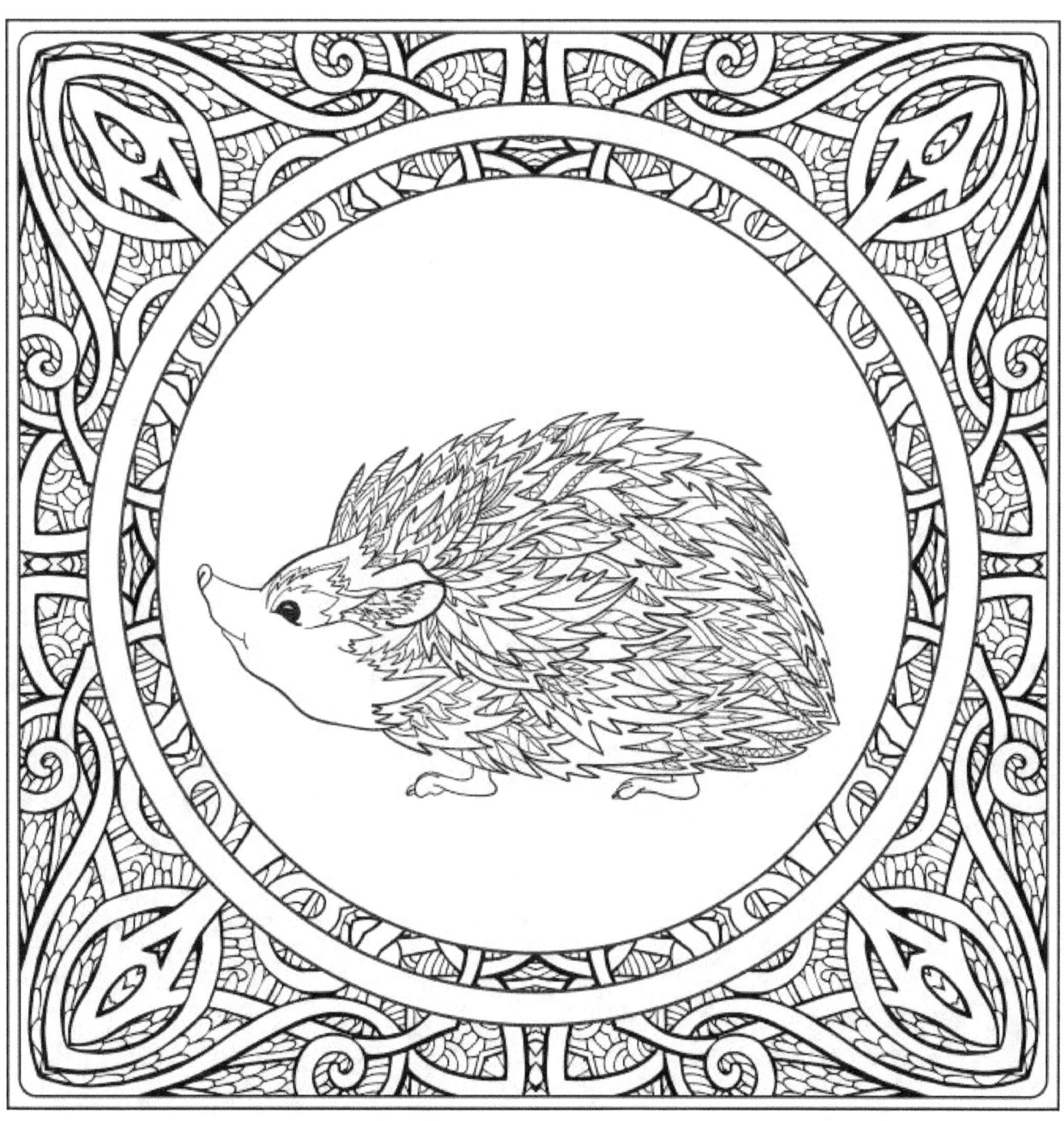

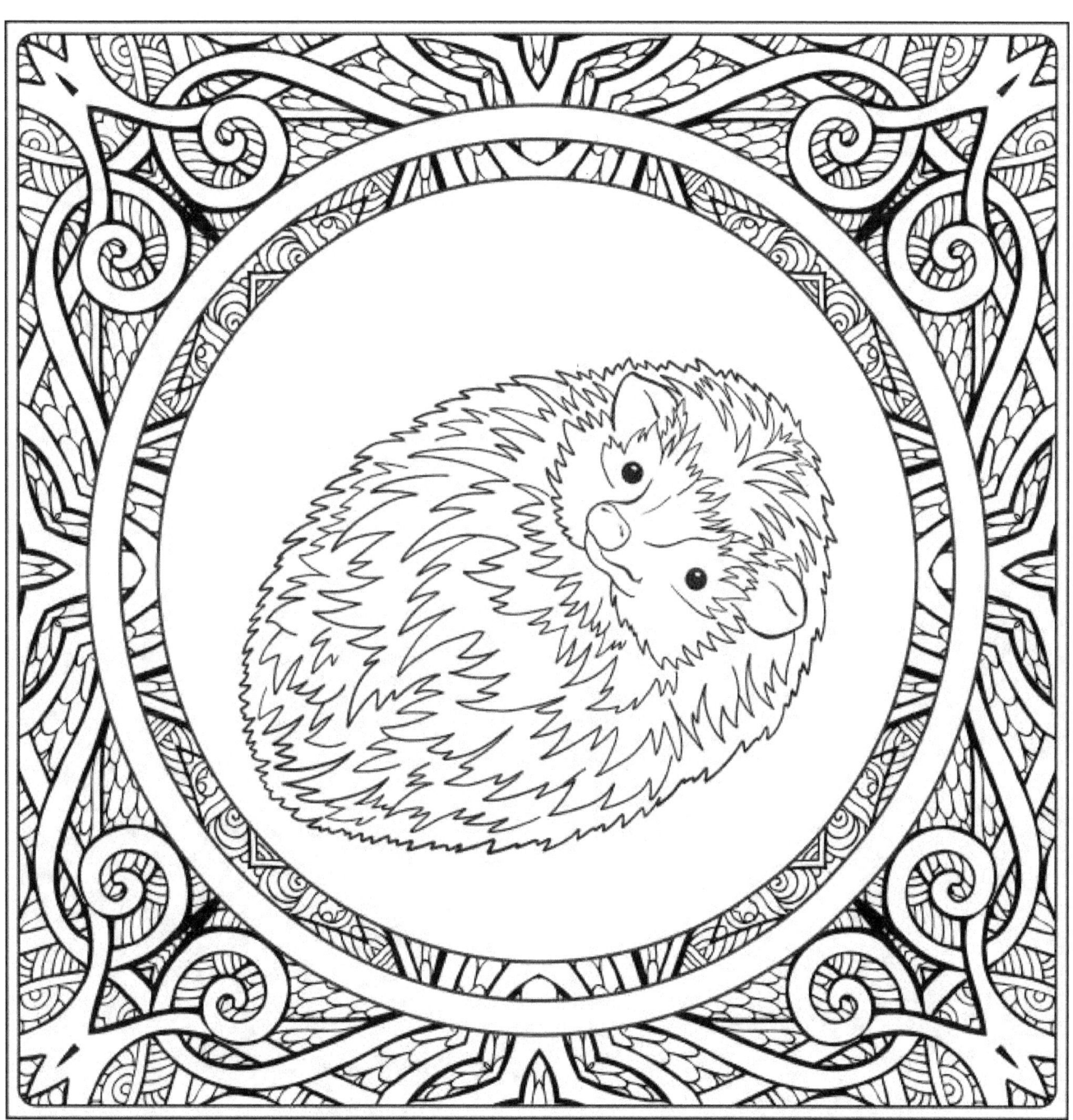

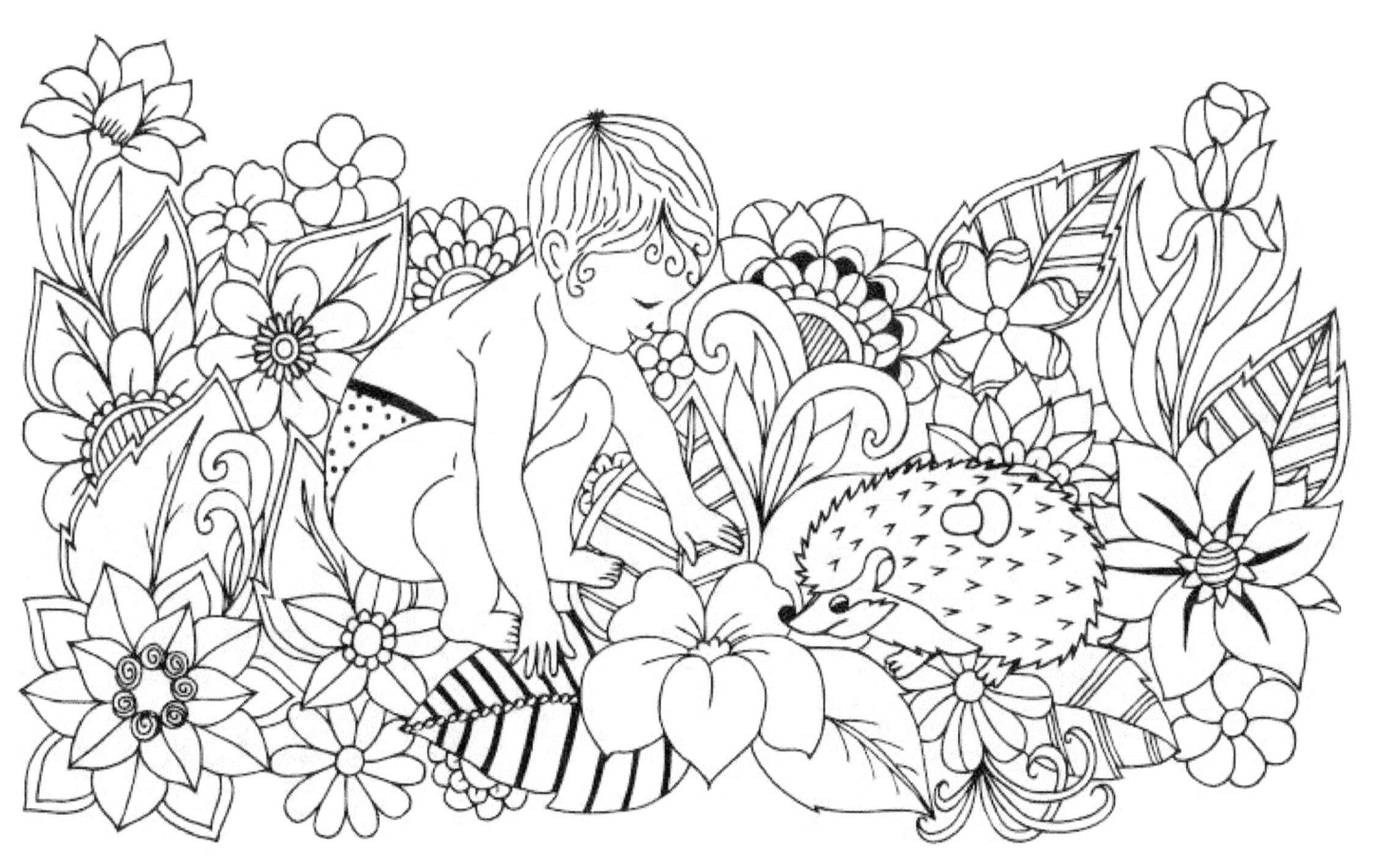

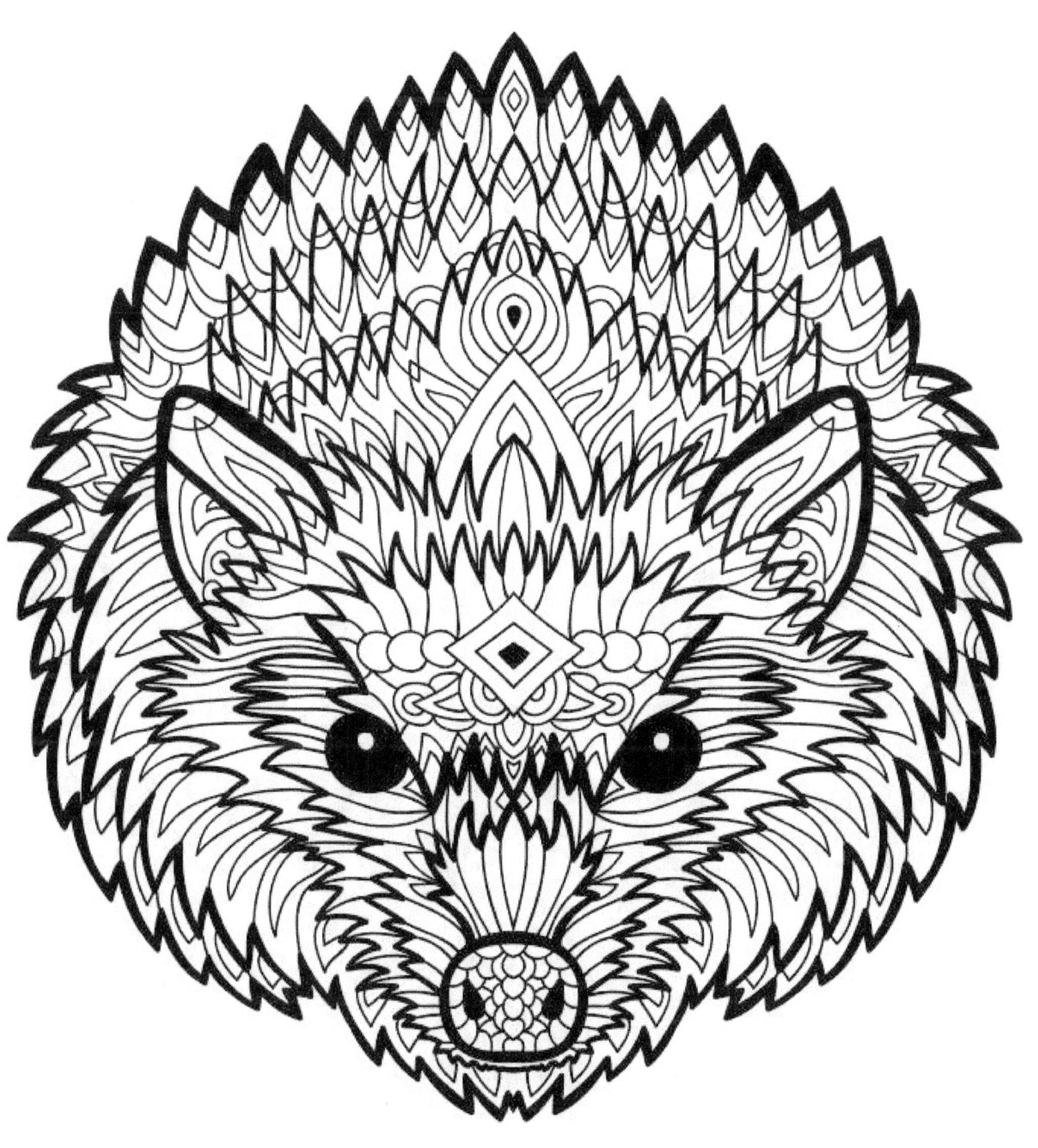

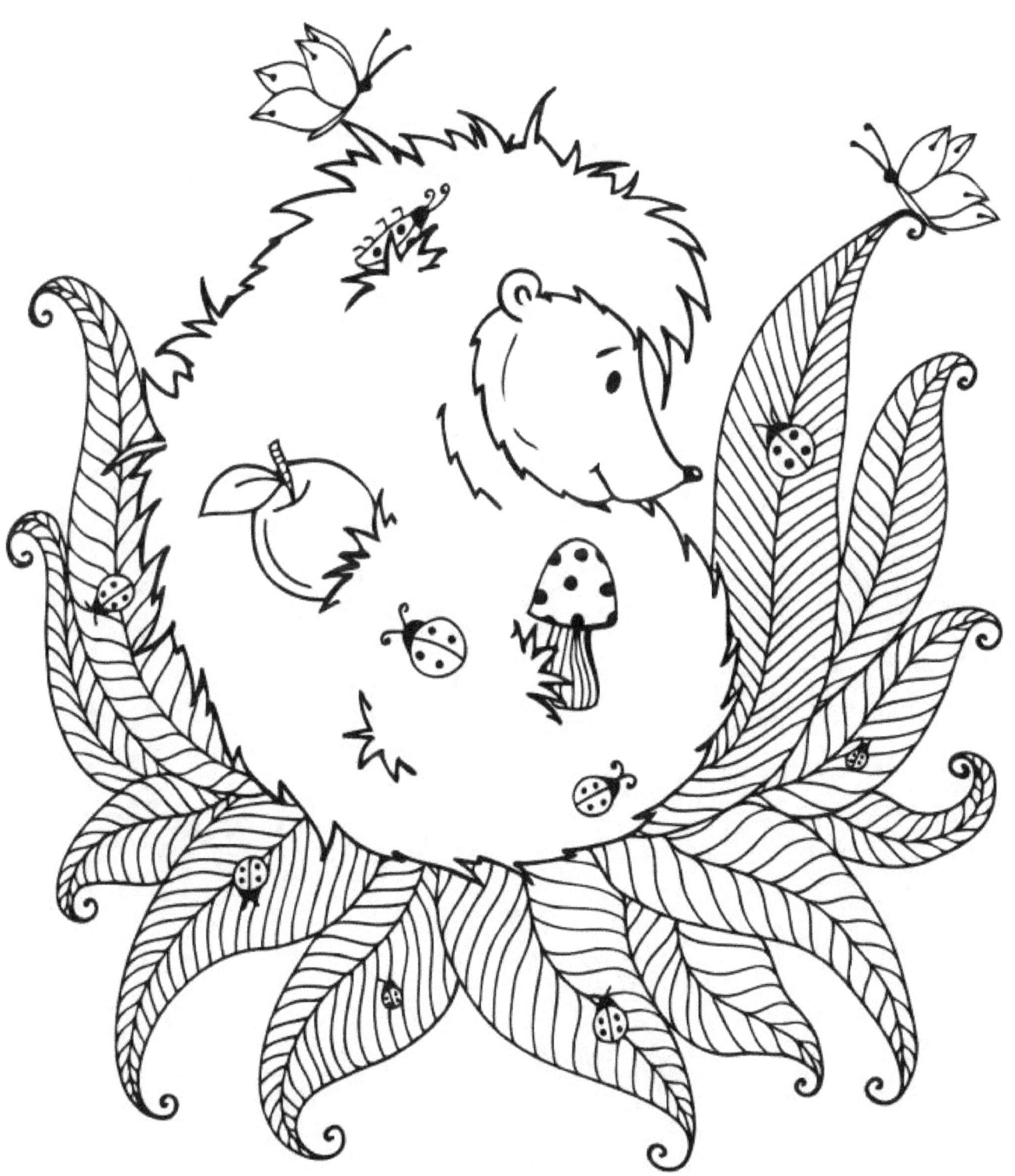

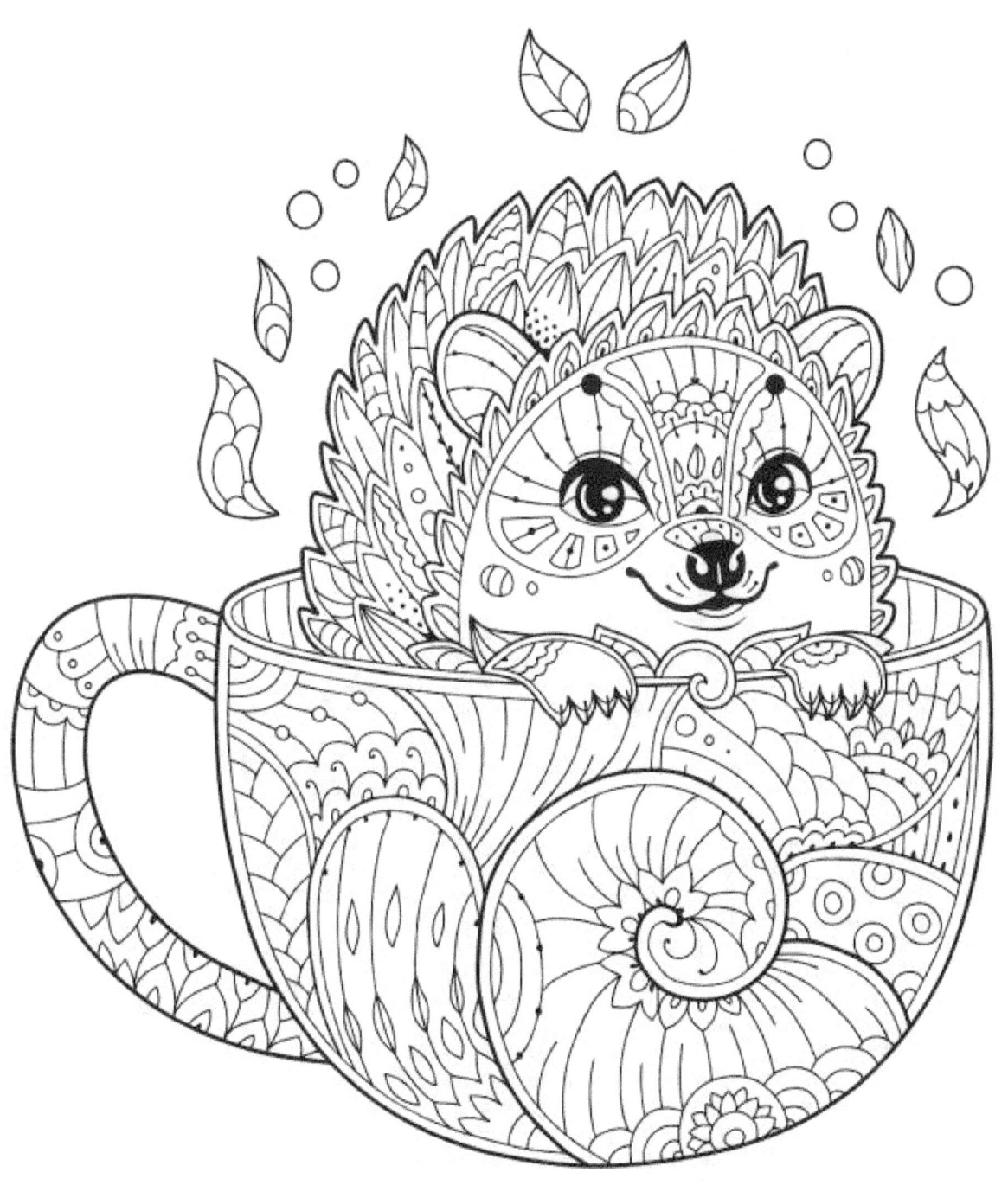

Surprise Bonus Turtle Coloring Illustrations for you to enjoy!

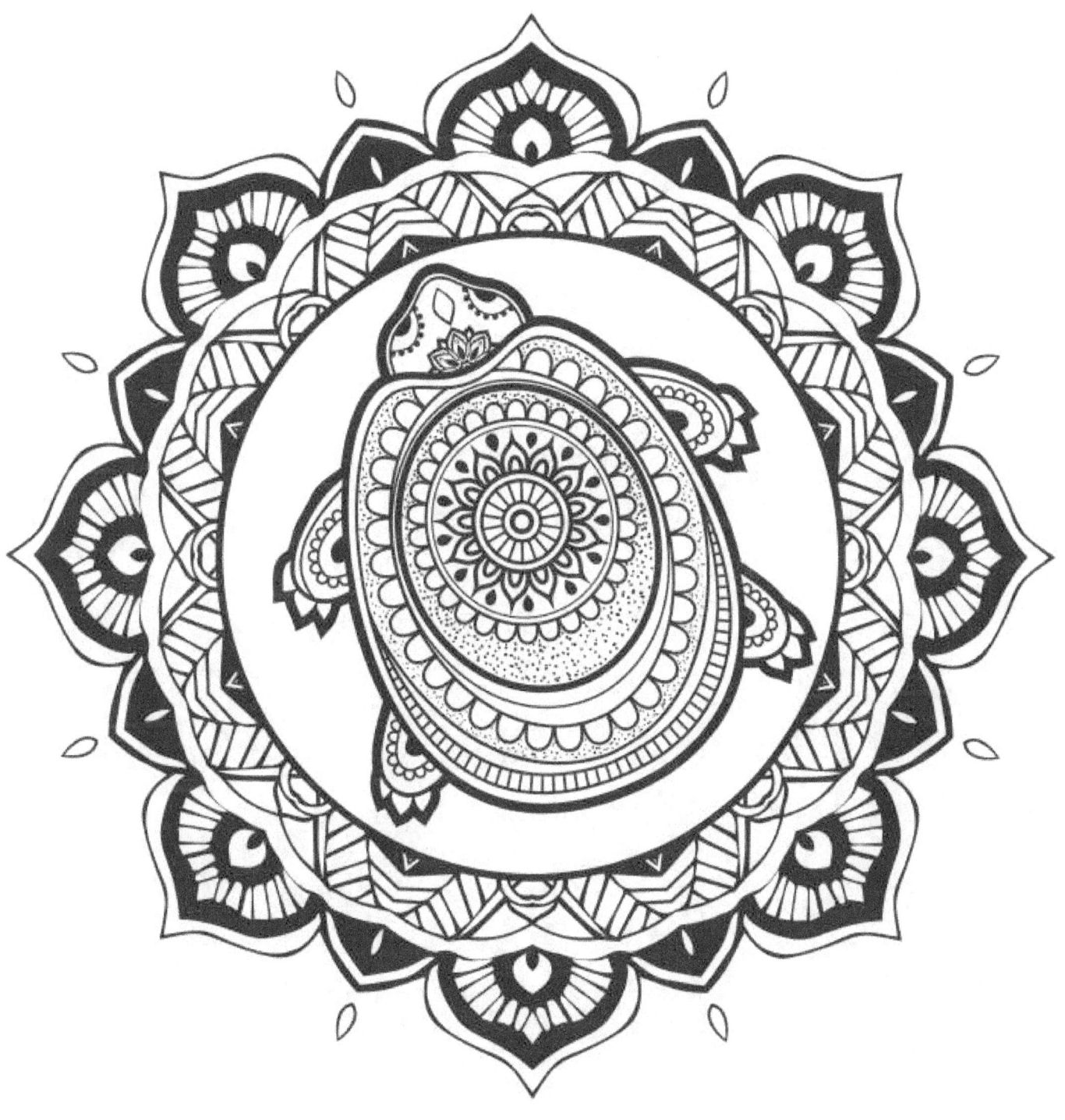

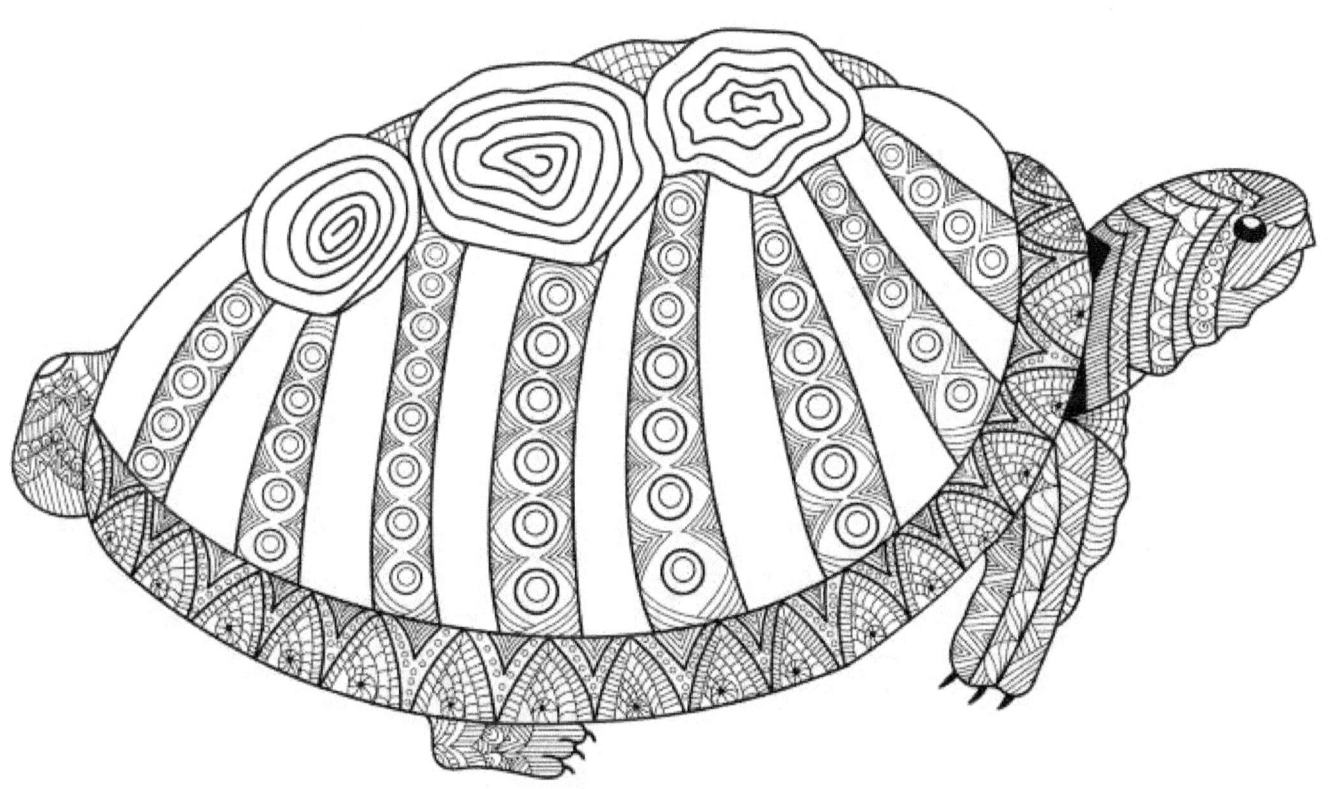

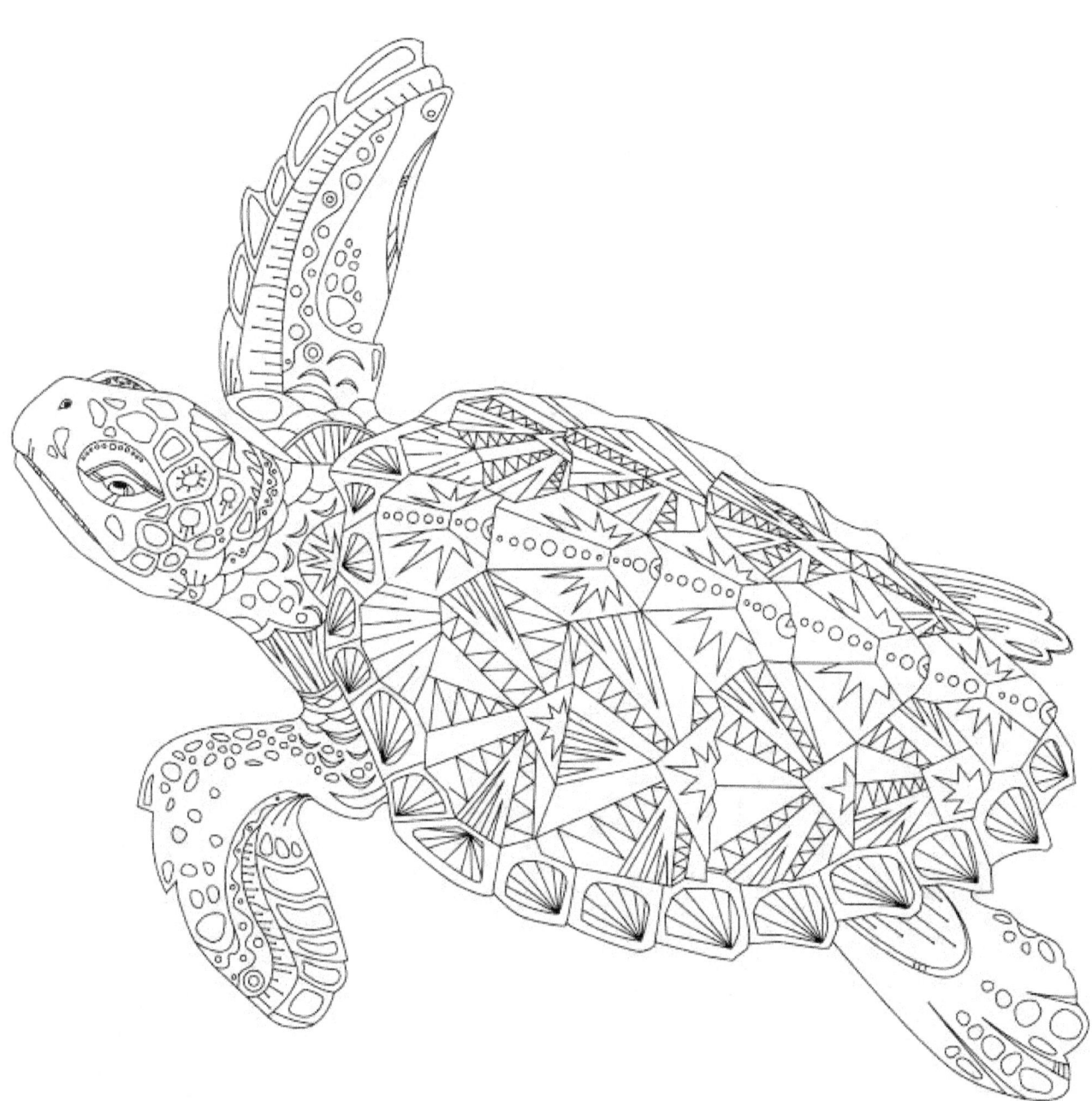

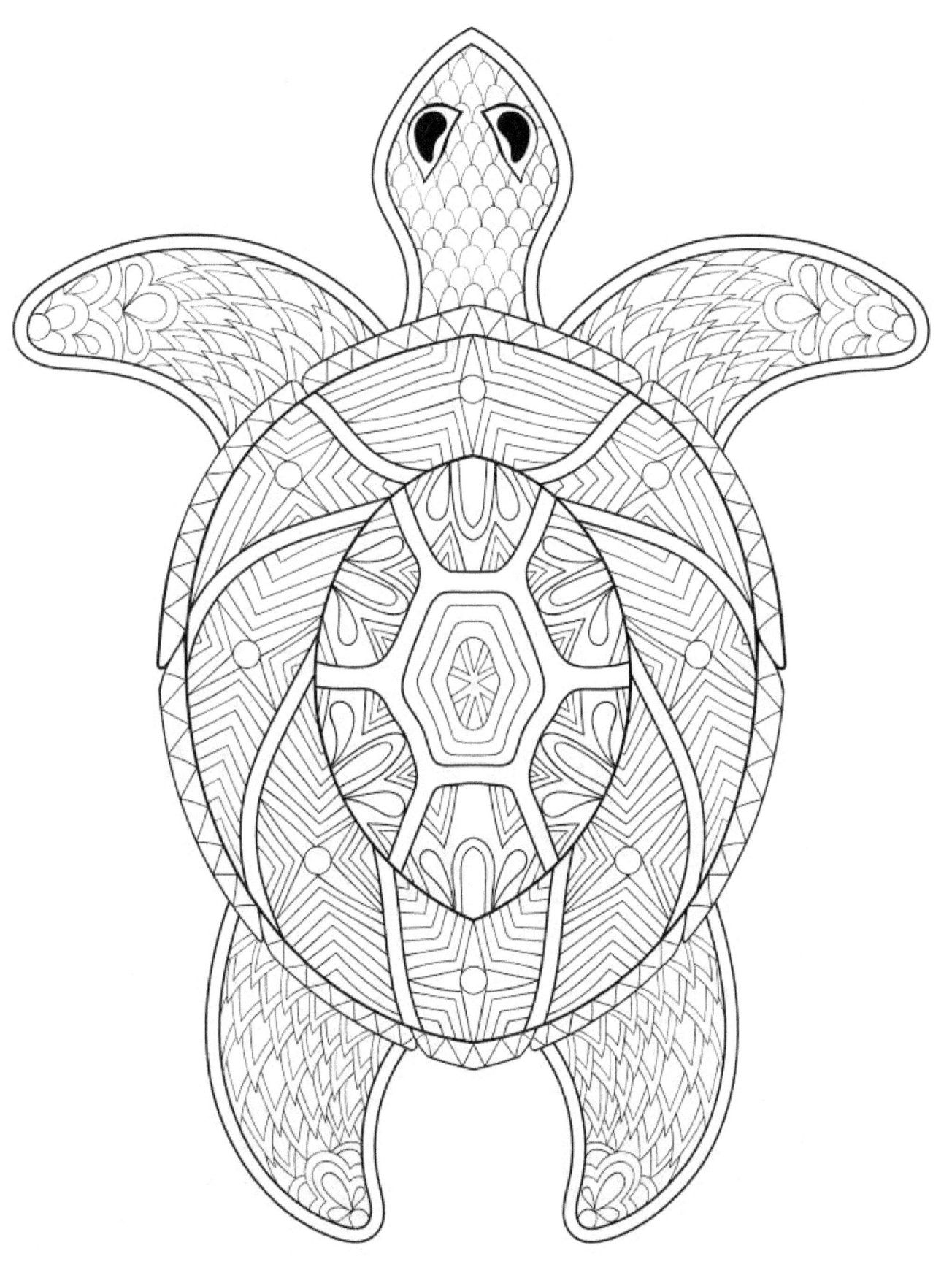

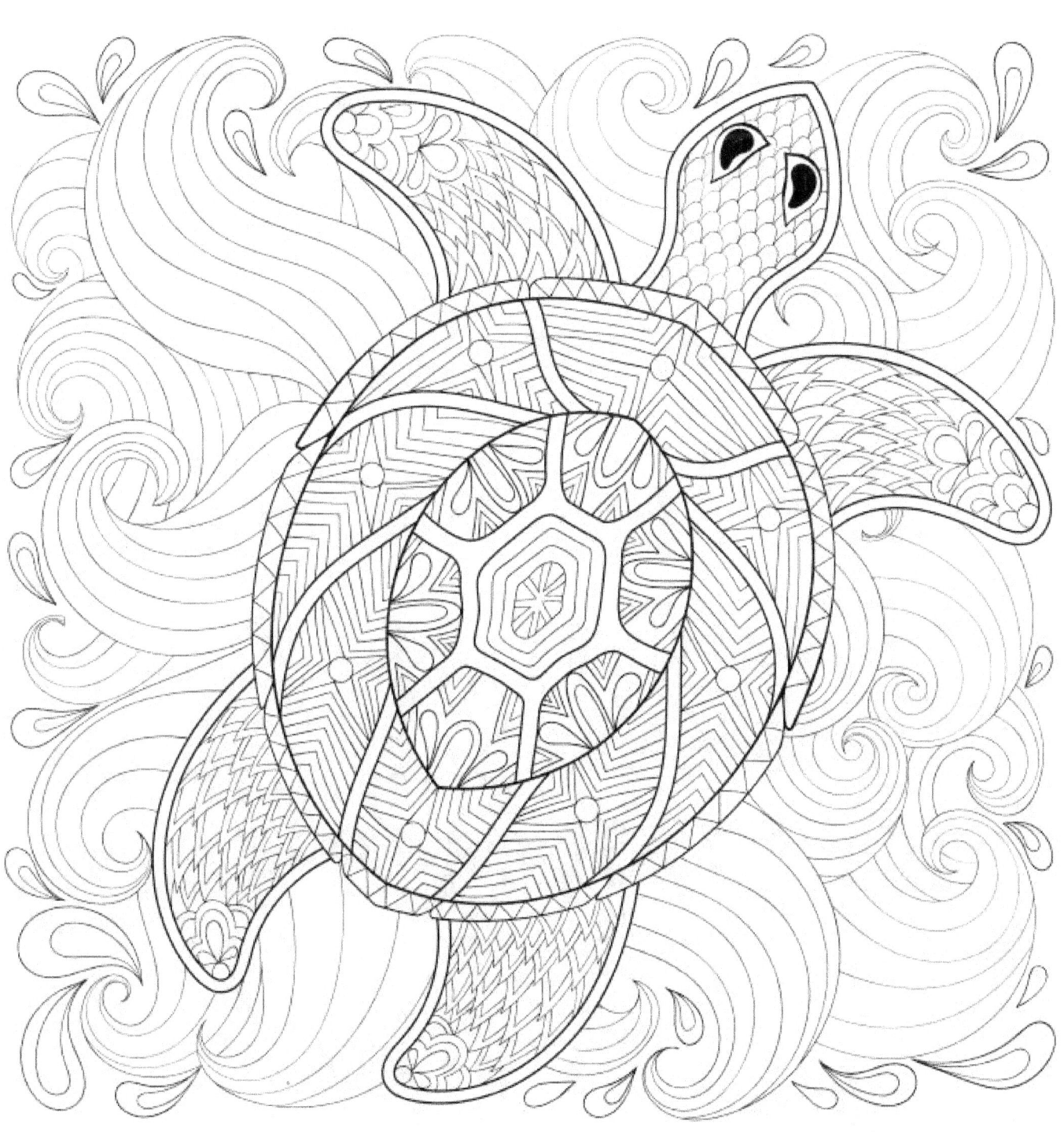

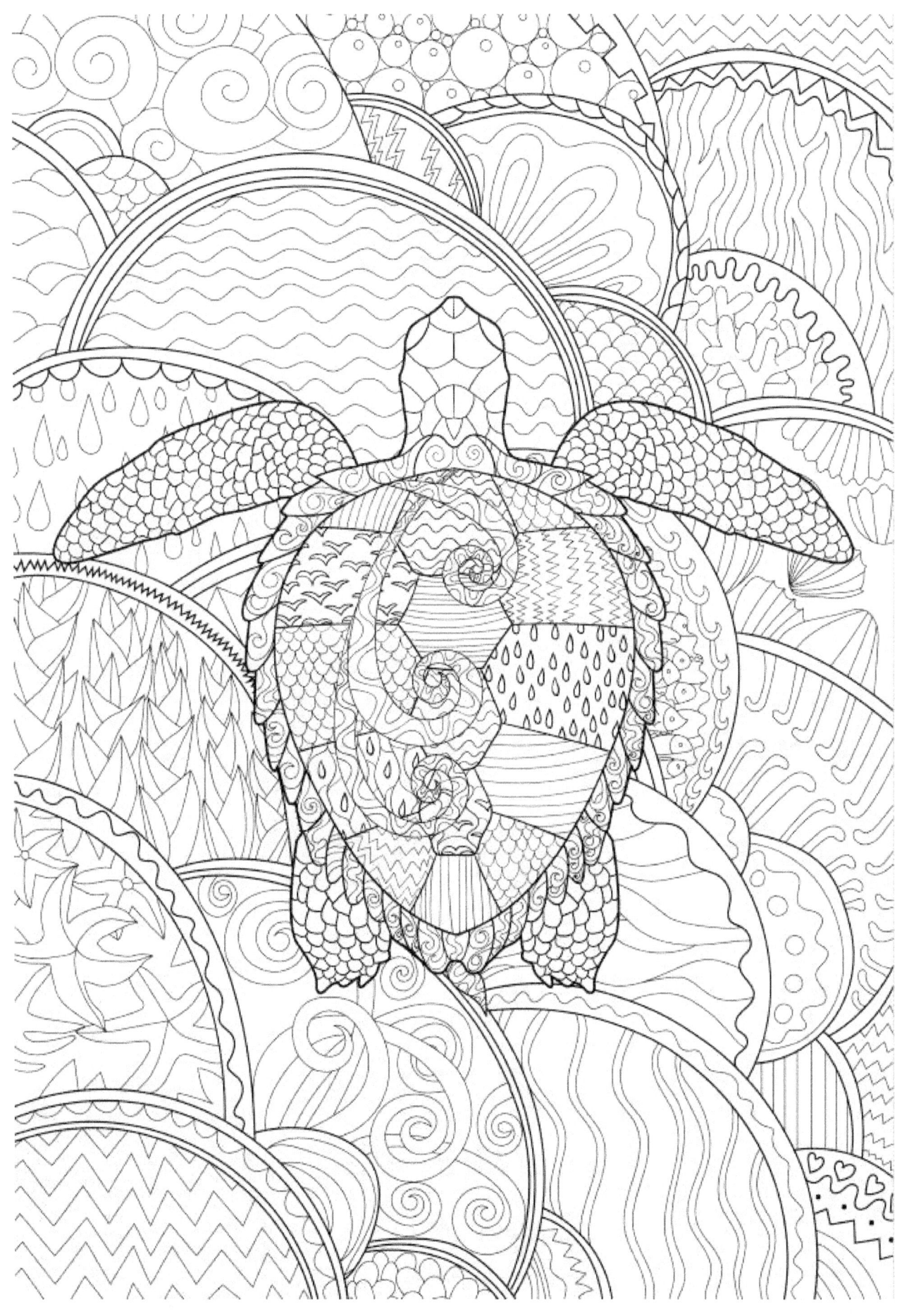

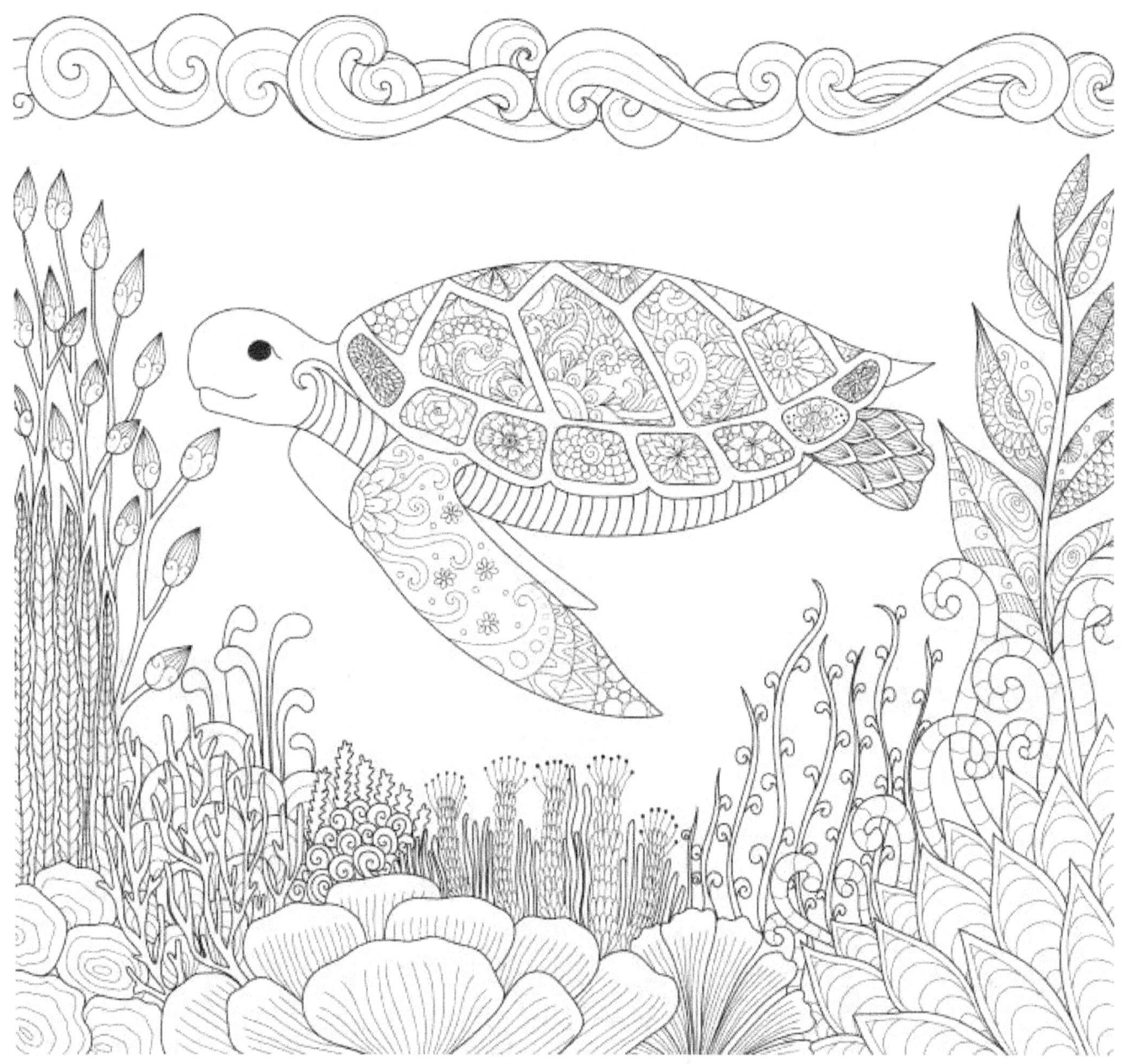

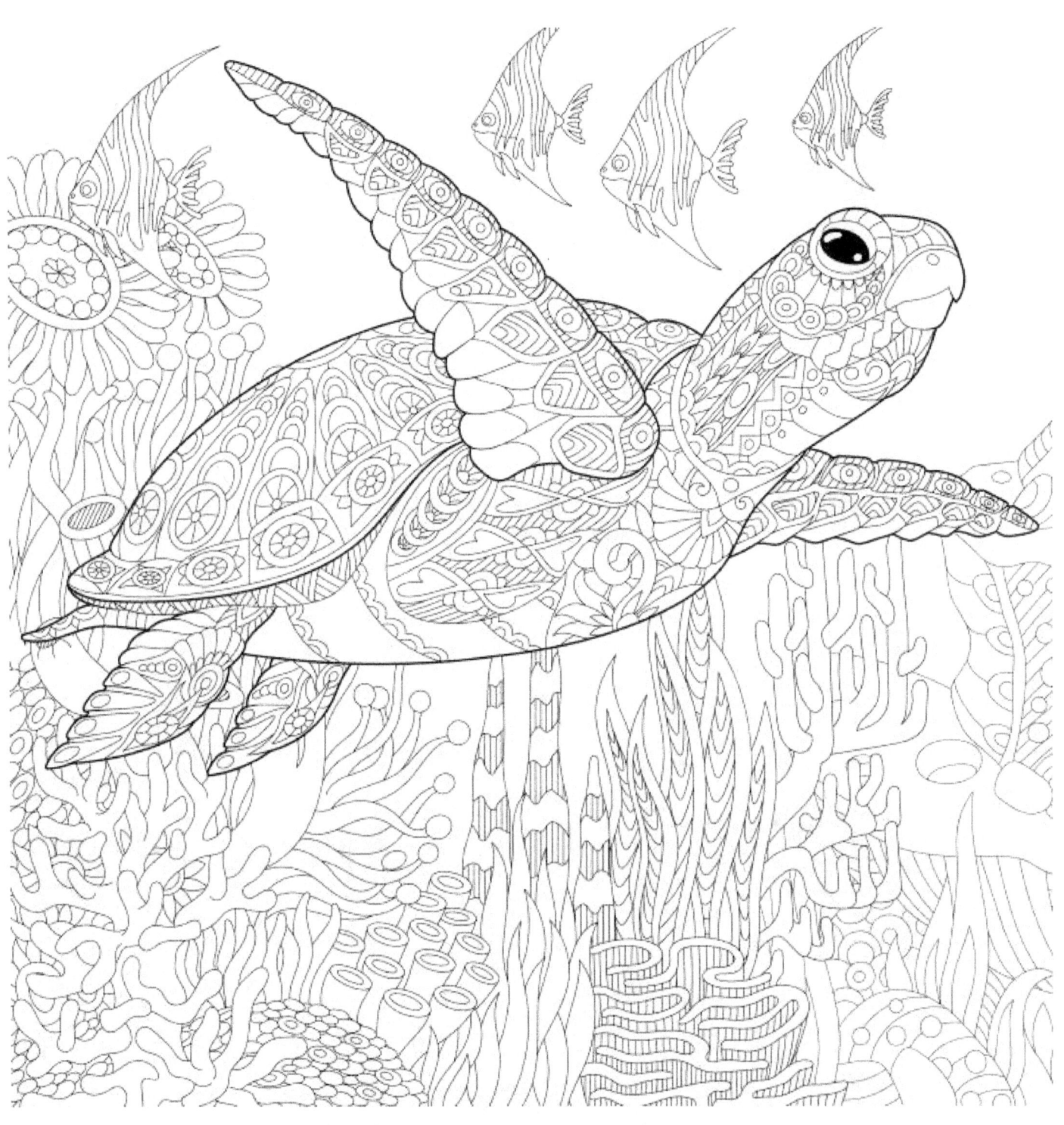

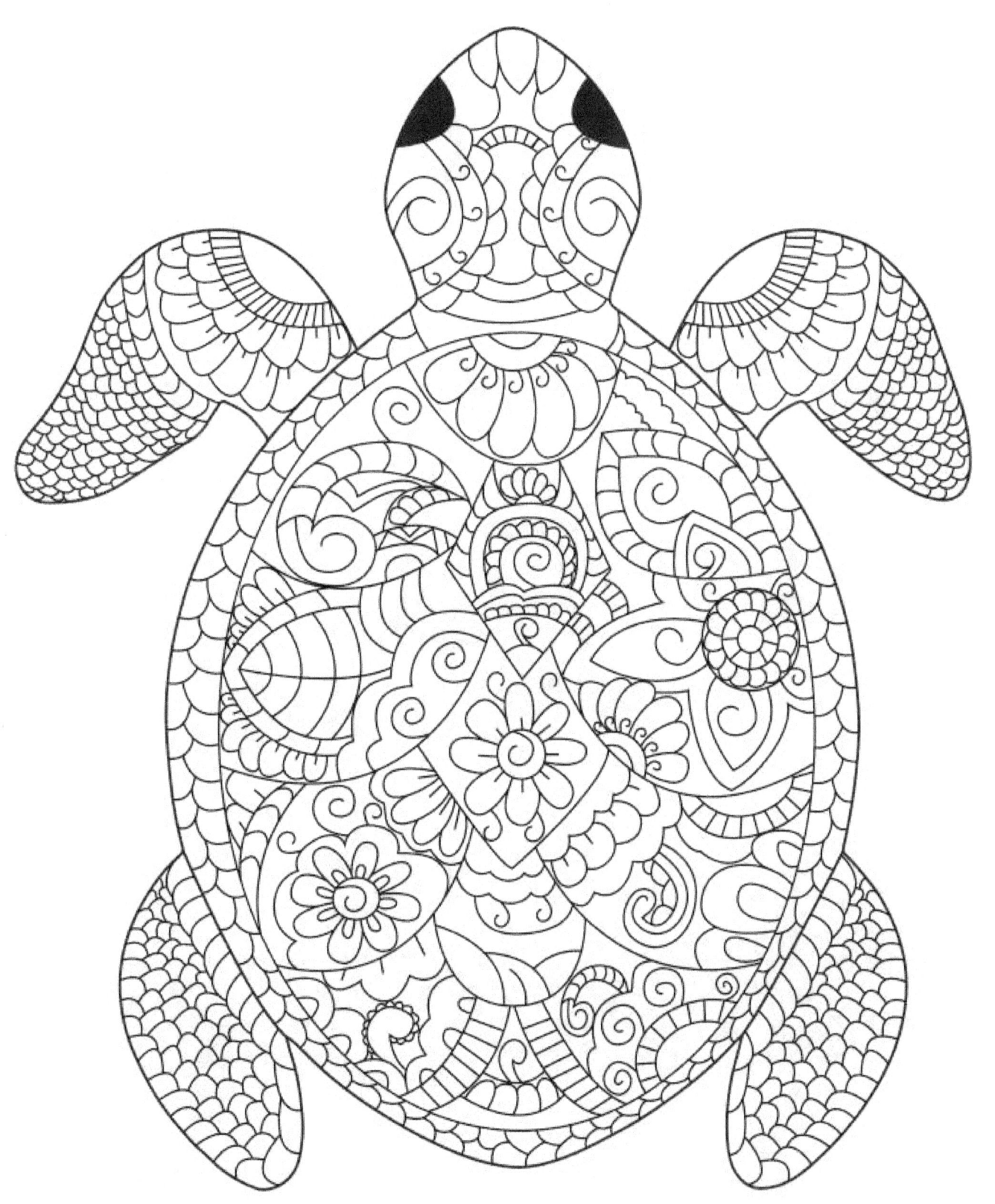

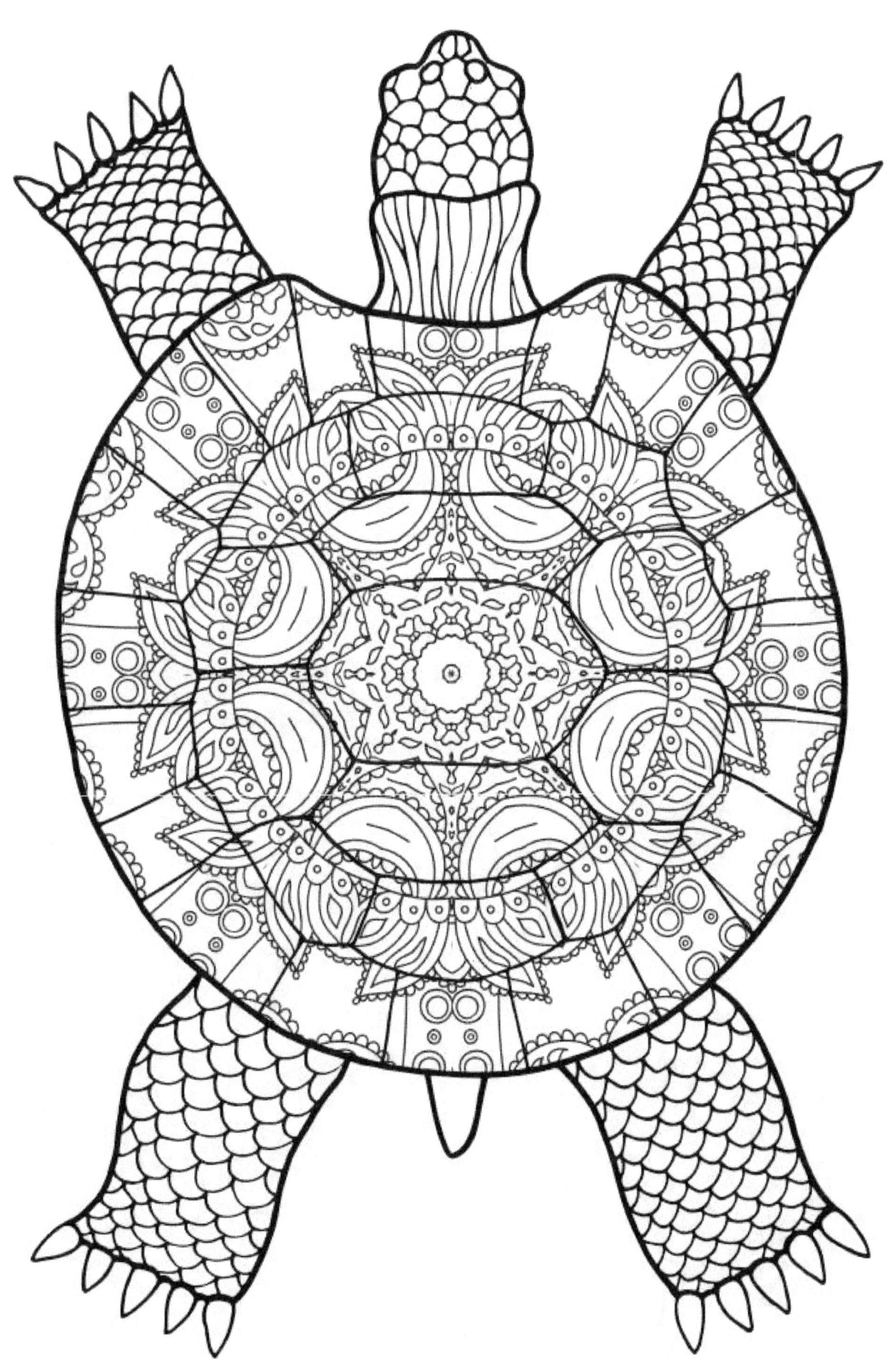

www.ingramcontent.com/pod-product-compliance
Lightning Source LLC
Chambersburg PA
CBHW081752170526
45167CB00009B/4002